We Need Nurses

by Lola M. Schaefer

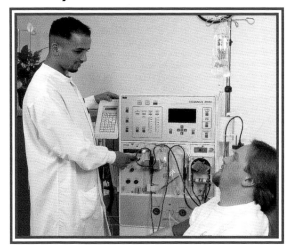

Consulting Editor: Gail Saunders-Smith, Ph.D.

Consultant: Denise M. Jordan, MA, RN
Instructor of Practical Nursing
Ivy Tech State College, Indiana

Pebble Books

an imprint of Capstone Press
Mankato, Minnesota

Pebble Books are published by Capstone Press
818 North Willow Street, Mankato, Minnesota 56001
http://www.capstone-press.com

Library of Congress Cataloging-in-Publication Data
Schaefer, Lola M., 1950–
    We need nurses/by Lola M. Schaefer.
    p. cm.—(Helpers in our community)
    Includes bibliographical references and index.
    Summary: Simple text and photographs present nurses and their role in
the community.
    ISBN 0-7368-0393-9
    1. Nursing—Juvenile literature. 2. Nurses—Juvenile literature. [1. Nurses
2. Nursing 3. Occupations.] I. Title. II. Series: Schaefer, Lola M., 1950– Helpers in
our community.
RT82.S38 2000
610.73'06'9—DC21   99-18415
                                                                                  CIP

Note to Parents and Teachers

The Helpers in Our Community series supports national social studies standards for units related to community helpers and their roles. This book describes and illustrates nurses and how they help people. The photographs support early readers in understanding the text. The repetition of words and phrases helps early readers learn new words. This book also introduces early readers to subject-specific vocabulary words, which are defined in the Words to Know section. Early readers may need assistance to read some words and to use the Table of Contents, Words to Know, Read More, Internet Sites, and Index/Word List sections of the book.

Table of Contents

A nurse helps people stay healthy.

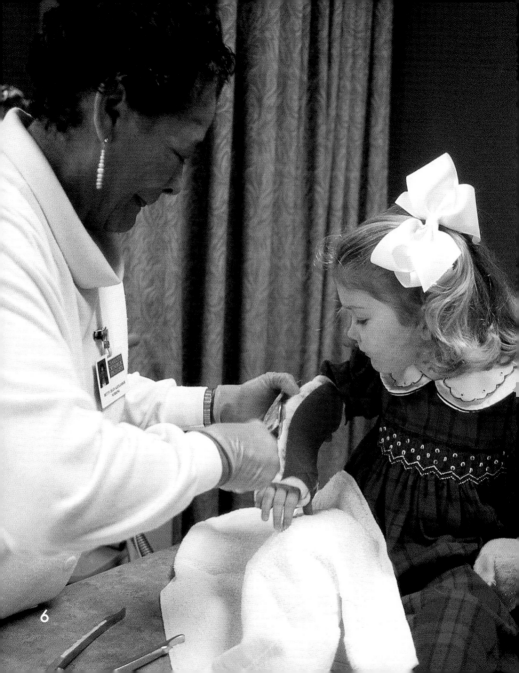

A nurse cares for people who are sick or hurt.

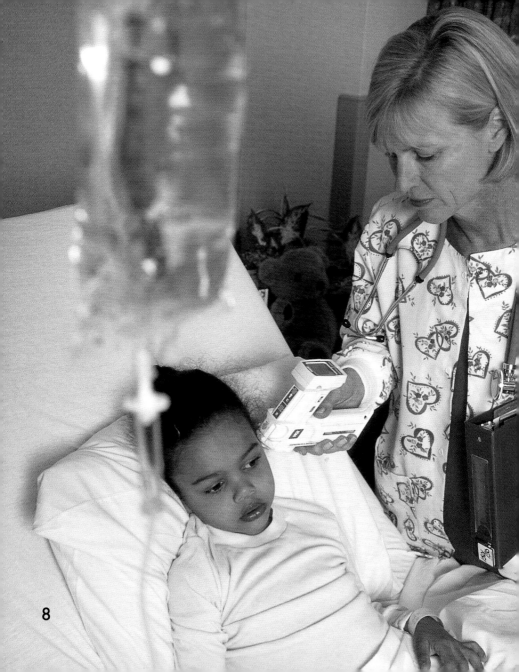

A nurse checks
a patient's temperature.

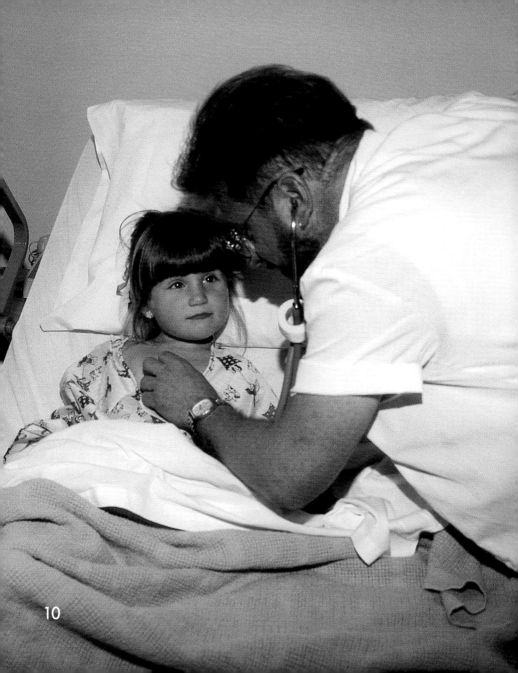

A nurse checks
a patient's heart.

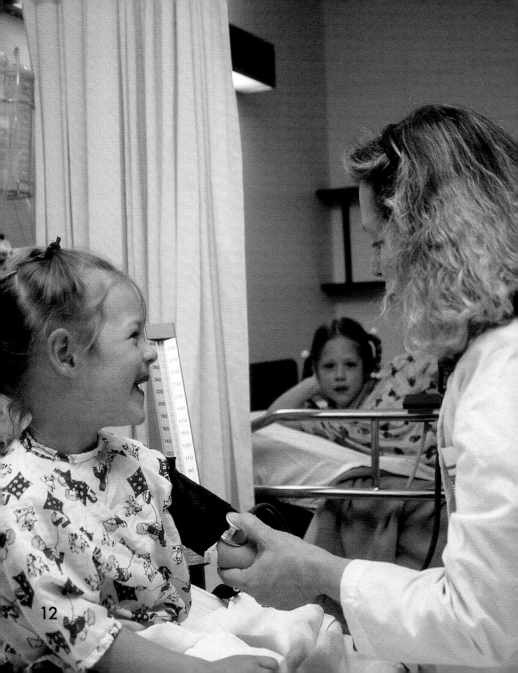

12

A nurse checks
a patient's blood pressure.

A nurse writes notes
on a patient's chart.

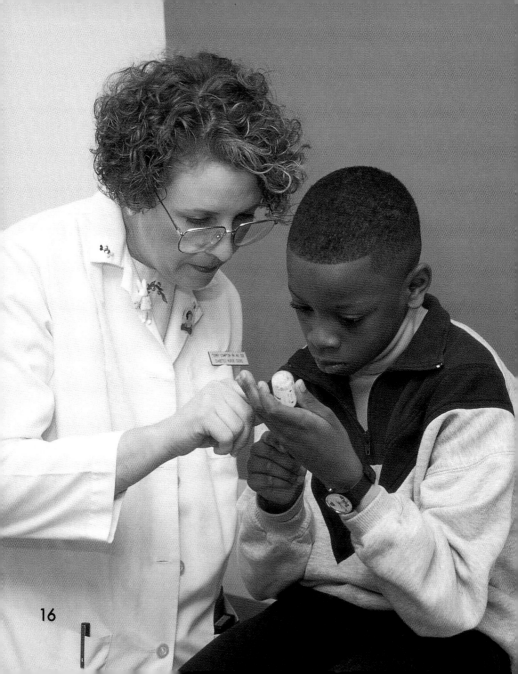

A nurse teaches a patient about medicine.

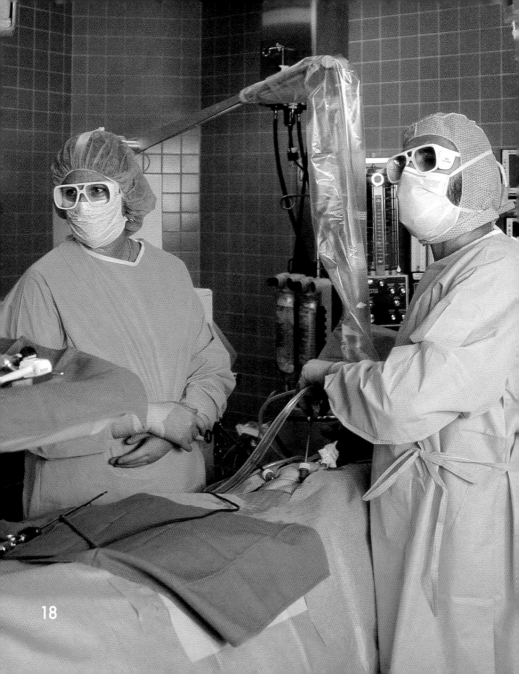

18

A nurse helps a doctor during surgery.

A nurse helps a doctor care for patients.

Words to Know

blood pressure—the force of blood as it flows through a person's body; a blood pressure test tells how hard and fast a person's heart is beating.

chart—facts kept about a patient's health; a nurse records a patient's heart rate, blood pressure, temperature, and medicine on a chart; charts let other health care workers know how a patient is doing.

medicine—drugs that help sick people get better; nurses give medicine to patients under their care.

patient—a person who receives medical care

surgery—repairing or removing body parts that are sick or hurt

temperature—how hot or cold something is; the average person has a body temperature of 98.6 degrees Fahrenheit (37 degrees Celsius).

Read More

Flanagan, Alice K. *Ask Nurse Pfaff, She'll Help You!* Our Neighborhood. New York: Children's Press, 1997.

James, Robert. *Nurses.* People Who Care for Our Health. Vero Beach, Fla.: Rourke, 1995.

Ready, Dee. *Nurses.* Community Helpers. Mankato, Minn.: Bridgestone Books, 1997.

Internet Sites

Fitness for Kids
http://www.fitnesslink.com/changes/kids.htm

Kids Health
http://kidshealth.org/kid/index.html

Yucky Gross & Cool Body
http://www.yucky.com/body

Index/Word List

Word Count: 65
Early-Intervention Level: 8

Editorial Credits
Karen L. Daas, editor; Abby Bradford, Bradfordesign, Inc., cover designer; Kimberly Danger, photo researcher

Photo Credits
David F. Clobes, cover
Index Stock Imagery, 6, 16; Index Stock Imagery/Jay Daniel, 1
International Stock/Michael J. Howell, 18
Leslie O'Shaughnessy, 10, 12
Ron Chapple/FPG International LLC, 4
Uniphoto, 8, 20; Uniphoto/Charles Gupton, 14